Caring for someone with **Autism** is often a stressful, ever-changing experience, and will differ from child to child.

The behavior of children with Autism can often be seen as random and uncontrollable. However, having up to date, accurate information about your child or patient can often lead to the identification of patterns and triggers, that help to ease to caring process. With this information, you will be better equipped to deal with these behaviors and health problems.

This note-keeping journal has been developed for the care of Autistic children on all levels of the spectrum, with notes for all the key aspects of this social disability. It is designed to track the daily and weekly needs and patterns, and help to establish the most efficient and effective care process.

With the daily logs, you track things like mood, activities and treatment, positives and negatives, and all other key information needed for a caregiver. Then, with the weekly recap, you are asked to summarise and more importantly look for patterns that will ultimately assist you in giving the best care you can. These patterns may come in the form of triggers, moods at different times of day and what causes them, and what has been working.

By spending a few minutes each day analyzing these aspects, you will eventually be able to save time and stress by only doing what is working, and avoiding what is not. It is important to note that children with Autism will change over time, some more rapidly than others, but by keeping a journal or logbook, these patterns will be able to be swiftly noticed, and caring routines will be able to be adapted to these changing needs.

USING THIS BOOK

Track moods at different times of day. Use notes to identify triggers / reasons if possible

Date

MOOD	TIME(S)	NOTES
☐ Happy		
☐ Grumpy		
☐ Tired		
☐ Energetic		
☐ Frustrated		
☐ Confused		
☐ Calm		
☐ Quiet		
☐ Restless		
☐ Anger		
☐ Anxious		
☐ Fearful		
☐ Other		

CARE NEEDS	TIME	CARE NEEDS	TIME
Needed Help		Did themselves	

What did they / didn't they need help with (E.g. bathroom, feeding). This may change over time

Non-essential tasks or activities that were successful or unsuccessful. Find patterns and develop care routines.

Keep notes of medication effects or side effects. Also keep notes or questions for next Doctor visit

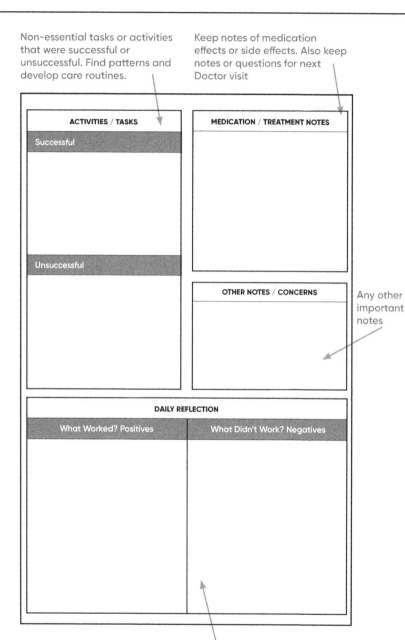

ACTIVITIES / TASKS

Successful

Unsuccessful

MEDICATION / TREATMENT NOTES

OTHER NOTES / CONCERNS

Any other important notes

DAILY REFLECTION

What Worked? Positives

What Didn't Work? Negatives

Reflection / Summary for the day. This is where you reflect on what worked and what didn't, and look for patterns that will assist you in improving your care routine.

Date

MOOD	TIME(S)	NOTES
☐ Happy		
☐ Grumpy		
☐ Tired		
☐ Energetic		
☐ Frustrated		
☐ Confused		
☐ Calm		
☐ Quiet		
☐ Restless		
☐ Anger		
☐ Anxious		
☐ Fearful		
☐ Other		

CARE NEEDS	TIME
Needed Help	

CARE NEEDS	TIME
Did themselves	

ACTIVITIES / TASKS

Successful

Unsuccessful

MEDICATION / TREATMENT NOTES

OTHER NOTES / CONCERNS

DAILY REFLECTION

What Worked? Positives	What Didn't Work? Negatives

Date

MOOD	TIME(S)	NOTES
☐ Happy		
☐ Grumpy		
☐ Tired		
☐ Energetic		
☐ Frustrated		
☐ Confused		
☐ Calm		
☐ Quiet		
☐ Restless		
☐ Anger		
☐ Anxious		
☐ Fearful		
☐ Other		

CARE NEEDS	TIME
Needed Help	

CARE NEEDS	TIME
Did themselves	

ACTIVITIES / TASKS	MEDICATION / TREATMENT NOTES
Successful	
Unsuccessful	
	OTHER NOTES / CONCERNS

DAILY REFLECTION	
What Worked? Positives	**What Didn't Work? Negatives**

Date

MOOD	TIME(S)	NOTES
☐ Happy		
☐ Grumpy		
☐ Tired		
☐ Energetic		
☐ Frustrated		
☐ Confused		
☐ Calm		
☐ Quiet		
☐ Restless		
☐ Anger		
☐ Anxious		
☐ Fearful		
☐ Other		

CARE NEEDS	TIME		CARE NEEDS	TIME
Needed Help			Did themselves	

ACTIVITIES / TASKS

Successful

Unsuccessful

MEDICATION / TREATMENT NOTES

OTHER NOTES / CONCERNS

DAILY REFLECTION

What Worked? Positives	What Didn't Work? Negatives

Date

MOOD	TIME(S)	NOTES
☐ Happy		
☐ Grumpy		
☐ Tired		
☐ Energetic		
☐ Frustrated		
☐ Confused		
☐ Calm		
☐ Quiet		
☐ Restless		
☐ Anger		
☐ Anxious		
☐ Fearful		
☐ Other		

CARE NEEDS	TIME
Needed Help	

CARE NEEDS	TIME
Did themselves	

ACTIVITIES / TASKS	MEDICATION / TREATMENT NOTES
Successful	
Unsuccessful	

OTHER NOTES / CONCERNS

DAILY REFLECTION

What Worked? Positives	What Didn't Work? Negatives

Date

MOOD	TIME(S)	NOTES
☐ Happy		
☐ Grumpy		
☐ Tired		
☐ Energetic		
☐ Frustrated		
☐ Confused		
☐ Calm		
☐ Quiet		
☐ Restless		
☐ Anger		
☐ Anxious		
☐ Fearful		
☐ Other		

CARE NEEDS	TIME
Needed Help	

CARE NEEDS	TIME
Did themselves	

ACTIVITIES / TASKS	MEDICATION / TREATMENT NOTES
Successful	
Unsuccessful	
	OTHER NOTES / CONCERNS

DAILY REFLECTION	
What Worked? Positives	**What Didn't Work? Negatives**

Date

MOOD	TIME(S)	NOTES
☐ Happy		
☐ Grumpy		
☐ Tired		
☐ Energetic		
☐ Frustrated		
☐ Confused		
☐ Calm		
☐ Quiet		
☐ Restless		
☐ Anger		
☐ Anxious		
☐ Fearful		
☐ Other		

CARE NEEDS	TIME
Needed Help	

CARE NEEDS	TIME
Did themselves	

ACTIVITIES / TASKS

Successful

Unsuccessful

MEDICATION / TREATMENT NOTES

OTHER NOTES / CONCERNS

DAILY REFLECTION

What Worked? Positives	What Didn't Work? Negatives

Date

MOOD	TIME(S)	NOTES
☐ Happy		
☐ Grumpy		
☐ Tired		
☐ Energetic		
☐ Frustrated		
☐ Confused		
☐ Calm		
☐ Quiet		
☐ Restless		
☐ Anger		
☐ Anxious		
☐ Fearful		
☐ Other		

CARE NEEDS	TIME
Needed Help	

CARE NEEDS	TIME
Did themselves	

ACTIVITIES / TASKS	MEDICATION / TREATMENT NOTES
Successful	
Unsuccessful	
	OTHER NOTES / CONCERNS

DAILY REFLECTION	
What Worked? Positives	What Didn't Work? Negatives

Weekly Recap & Patterns

MAIN MOOD(S) / TIMES / PATTERNS

CARE NEEDS PATTERNS

Needed Help

Did Themselves

WEEKLY ACTIVITIES / TASK PATTERNS

Successful

Unsuccessful

MEDICATION / TREATMENT NOTES

OTHER NOTES / WEEKLY CONCERNS

WEEKLY REFLECTION

What Worked? Positives	What Didn't Work? Negatives

Date

MOOD	TIME(S)	NOTES
☐ Happy		
☐ Grumpy		
☐ Tired		
☐ Energetic		
☐ Frustrated		
☐ Confused		
☐ Calm		
☐ Quiet		
☐ Restless		
☐ Anger		
☐ Anxious		
☐ Fearful		
☐ Other		

CARE NEEDS	TIME
Needed Help	

CARE NEEDS	TIME
Did themselves	

ACTIVITIES / TASKS	MEDICATION / TREATMENT NOTES
Successful	
Unsuccessful	

OTHER NOTES / CONCERNS

DAILY REFLECTION	
What Worked? Positives	**What Didn't Work? Negatives**

Date

MOOD	TIME(S)	NOTES
☐ Happy		
☐ Grumpy		
☐ Tired		
☐ Energetic		
☐ Frustrated		
☐ Confused		
☐ Calm		
☐ Quiet		
☐ Restless		
☐ Anger		
☐ Anxious		
☐ Fearful		
☐ Other		

CARE NEEDS	TIME
Needed Help	

CARE NEEDS	TIME
Did themselves	

ACTIVITIES / TASKS

Successful

Unsuccessful

MEDICATION / TREATMENT NOTES

OTHER NOTES / CONCERNS

DAILY REFLECTION

What Worked? Positives	What Didn't Work? Negatives

Date

MOOD	TIME(S)	NOTES
☐ Happy		
☐ Grumpy		
☐ Tired		
☐ Energetic		
☐ Frustrated		
☐ Confused		
☐ Calm		
☐ Quiet		
☐ Restless		
☐ Anger		
☐ Anxious		
☐ Fearful		
☐ Other		

CARE NEEDS	TIME
Needed Help	

CARE NEEDS	TIME
Did themselves	

ACTIVITIES / TASKS	MEDICATION / TREATMENT NOTES
Successful	
Unsuccessful	**OTHER NOTES / CONCERNS**

DAILY REFLECTION	
What Worked? Positives	**What Didn't Work? Negatives**

Date

MOOD	TIME(S)	NOTES
☐ Happy		
☐ Grumpy		
☐ Tired		
☐ Energetic		
☐ Frustrated		
☐ Confused		
☐ Calm		
☐ Quiet		
☐ Restless		
☐ Anger		
☐ Anxious		
☐ Fearful		
☐ Other		

CARE NEEDS	TIME		CARE NEEDS	TIME
Needed Help			Did themselves	

ACTIVITIES / TASKS	MEDICATION / TREATMENT NOTES
Successful	
Unsuccessful	

OTHER NOTES / CONCERNS

DAILY REFLECTION	
What Worked? Positives	**What Didn't Work? Negatives**

Date

MOOD	TIME(S)	NOTES
☐ Happy		
☐ Grumpy		
☐ Tired		
☐ Energetic		
☐ Frustrated		
☐ Confused		
☐ Calm		
☐ Quiet		
☐ Restless		
☐ Anger		
☐ Anxious		
☐ Fearful		
☐ Other		

CARE NEEDS	TIME
Needed Help	

CARE NEEDS	TIME
Did themselves	

ACTIVITIES / TASKS

Successful

Unsuccessful

MEDICATION / TREATMENT NOTES

OTHER NOTES / CONCERNS

DAILY REFLECTION

What Worked? Positives	What Didn't Work? Negatives

Date

MOOD	TIME(S)	NOTES
☐ Happy		
☐ Grumpy		
☐ Tired		
☐ Energetic		
☐ Frustrated		
☐ Confused		
☐ Calm		
☐ Quiet		
☐ Restless		
☐ Anger		
☐ Anxious		
☐ Fearful		
☐ Other		

CARE NEEDS	TIME	CARE NEEDS	TIME
Needed Help		Did themselves	

ACTIVITIES / TASKS

Successful

Unsuccessful

MEDICATION / TREATMENT NOTES

OTHER NOTES / CONCERNS

DAILY REFLECTION

What Worked? Positives	What Didn't Work? Negatives

Date

MOOD	TIME(S)	NOTES
☐ Happy		
☐ Grumpy		
☐ Tired		
☐ Energetic		
☐ Frustrated		
☐ Confused		
☐ Calm		
☐ Quiet		
☐ Restless		
☐ Anger		
☐ Anxious		
☐ Fearful		
☐ Other		

CARE NEEDS	TIME	CARE NEEDS	TIME
Needed Help		Did themselves	

ACTIVITIES / TASKS	MEDICATION / TREATMENT NOTES
Successful	
Unsuccessful	
	OTHER NOTES / CONCERNS

DAILY REFLECTION	
What Worked? Positives	**What Didn't Work? Negatives**

Weekly Recap & Patterns

MAIN MOOD(S) / TIMES / PATTERNS

CARE NEEDS PATTERNS
Needed Help
Did Themselves

WEEKLY ACTIVITIES / TASK PATTERNS	MEDICATION / TREATMENT NOTES
Successful	
Unsuccessful	**OTHER NOTES / WEEKLY CONCERNS**

WEEKLY REFLECTION	
What Worked? Positives	What Didn't Work? Negatives

Date

MOOD	TIME(S)	NOTES
☐ Happy		
☐ Grumpy		
☐ Tired		
☐ Energetic		
☐ Frustrated		
☐ Confused		
☐ Calm		
☐ Quiet		
☐ Restless		
☐ Anger		
☐ Anxious		
☐ Fearful		
☐ Other		

CARE NEEDS	TIME
Needed Help	

CARE NEEDS	TIME
Did themselves	

ACTIVITIES / TASKS

Successful

Unsuccessful

MEDICATION / TREATMENT NOTES

OTHER NOTES / CONCERNS

DAILY REFLECTION

What Worked? Positives	What Didn't Work? Negatives

Date

MOOD	TIME(S)	NOTES
☐ Happy		
☐ Grumpy		
☐ Tired		
☐ Energetic		
☐ Frustrated		
☐ Confused		
☐ Calm		
☐ Quiet		
☐ Restless		
☐ Anger		
☐ Anxious		
☐ Fearful		
☐ Other		

CARE NEEDS	TIME
Needed Help	

CARE NEEDS	TIME
Did themselves	

ACTIVITIES / TASKS	MEDICATION / TREATMENT NOTES
Successful	
Unsuccessful	
	OTHER NOTES / CONCERNS

DAILY REFLECTION	
What Worked? Positives	**What Didn't Work? Negatives**

Date

MOOD	TIME(S)	NOTES
☐ Happy		
☐ Grumpy		
☐ Tired		
☐ Energetic		
☐ Frustrated		
☐ Confused		
☐ Calm		
☐ Quiet		
☐ Restless		
☐ Anger		
☐ Anxious		
☐ Fearful		
☐ Other		

CARE NEEDS	TIME	CARE NEEDS	TIME
Needed Help		Did themselves	

ACTIVITIES / TASKS	MEDICATION / TREATMENT NOTES
Successful	
Unsuccessful	
	OTHER NOTES / CONCERNS

DAILY REFLECTION	
What Worked? Positives	What Didn't Work? Negatives

Date

MOOD	TIME(S)	NOTES
☐ Happy		
☐ Grumpy		
☐ Tired		
☐ Energetic		
☐ Frustrated		
☐ Confused		
☐ Calm		
☐ Quiet		
☐ Restless		
☐ Anger		
☐ Anxious		
☐ Fearful		
☐ Other		

CARE NEEDS	TIME
Needed Help	

CARE NEEDS	TIME
Did themselves	

ACTIVITIES / TASKS

Successful

Unsuccessful

MEDICATION / TREATMENT NOTES

OTHER NOTES / CONCERNS

DAILY REFLECTION

What Worked? Positives	What Didn't Work? Negatives

Date

MOOD	TIME(S)	NOTES
☐ Happy		
☐ Grumpy		
☐ Tired		
☐ Energetic		
☐ Frustrated		
☐ Confused		
☐ Calm		
☐ Quiet		
☐ Restless		
☐ Anger		
☐ Anxious		
☐ Fearful		
☐ Other		

CARE NEEDS	TIME
Needed Help	

CARE NEEDS	TIME
Did themselves	

ACTIVITIES / TASKS

Successful

Unsuccessful

MEDICATION / TREATMENT NOTES

OTHER NOTES / CONCERNS

DAILY REFLECTION

What Worked? Positives	What Didn't Work? Negatives

Date

MOOD	TIME(S)	NOTES
☐ Happy		
☐ Grumpy		
☐ Tired		
☐ Energetic		
☐ Frustrated		
☐ Confused		
☐ Calm		
☐ Quiet		
☐ Restless		
☐ Anger		
☐ Anxious		
☐ Fearful		
☐ Other		

CARE NEEDS	TIME
Needed Help	

CARE NEEDS	TIME
Did themselves	

ACTIVITIES / TASKS	MEDICATION / TREATMENT NOTES
Successful	
Unsuccessful	
	OTHER NOTES / CONCERNS

DAILY REFLECTION	
What Worked? Positives	What Didn't Work? Negatives

Date

MOOD	TIME(S)	NOTES
☐ Happy		
☐ Grumpy		
☐ Tired		
☐ Energetic		
☐ Frustrated		
☐ Confused		
☐ Calm		
☐ Quiet		
☐ Restless		
☐ Anger		
☐ Anxious		
☐ Fearful		
☐ Other		

CARE NEEDS	TIME		CARE NEEDS	TIME
Needed Help			Did themselves	

ACTIVITIES / TASKS

Successful

Unsuccessful

MEDICATION / TREATMENT NOTES

OTHER NOTES / CONCERNS

DAILY REFLECTION

What Worked? Positives

What Didn't Work? Negatives

Weekly Recap & Patterns

MAIN MOOD(S) / TIMES / PATTERNS

CARE NEEDS PATTERNS

Needed Help

Did Themselves

WEEKLY ACTIVITIES / TASK PATTERNS	MEDICATION / TREATMENT NOTES
Successful	
Unsuccessful	**OTHER NOTES / WEEKLY CONCERNS**

WEEKLY REFLECTION

What Worked? Positives	What Didn't Work? Negatives

Date

MOOD	TIME(S)	NOTES
☐ Happy		
☐ Grumpy		
☐ Tired		
☐ Energetic		
☐ Frustrated		
☐ Confused		
☐ Calm		
☐ Quiet		
☐ Restless		
☐ Anger		
☐ Anxious		
☐ Fearful		
☐ Other		

CARE NEEDS	TIME
Needed Help	

CARE NEEDS	TIME
Did themselves	

ACTIVITIES / TASKS

Successful

Unsuccessful

MEDICATION / TREATMENT NOTES

OTHER NOTES / CONCERNS

DAILY REFLECTION

What Worked? Positives	What Didn't Work? Negatives

Date

MOOD	TIME(S)	NOTES
☐ Happy		
☐ Grumpy		
☐ Tired		
☐ Energetic		
☐ Frustrated		
☐ Confused		
☐ Calm		
☐ Quiet		
☐ Restless		
☐ Anger		
☐ Anxious		
☐ Fearful		
☐ Other		

CARE NEEDS	TIME
Needed Help	

CARE NEEDS	TIME
Did themselves	

ACTIVITIES / TASKS

Successful

Unsuccessful

MEDICATION / TREATMENT NOTES

OTHER NOTES / CONCERNS

DAILY REFLECTION

What Worked? Positives	What Didn't Work? Negatives

Date

MOOD	TIME(S)	NOTES
☐ Happy		
☐ Grumpy		
☐ Tired		
☐ Energetic		
☐ Frustrated		
☐ Confused		
☐ Calm		
☐ Quiet		
☐ Restless		
☐ Anger		
☐ Anxious		
☐ Fearful		
☐ Other		

CARE NEEDS	TIME
Needed Help	

CARE NEEDS	TIME
Did themselves	

ACTIVITIES / TASKS

Successful

Unsuccessful

MEDICATION / TREATMENT NOTES

OTHER NOTES / CONCERNS

DAILY REFLECTION

What Worked? Positives	What Didn't Work? Negatives

Date

MOOD	TIME(S)	NOTES
☐ Happy		
☐ Grumpy		
☐ Tired		
☐ Energetic		
☐ Frustrated		
☐ Confused		
☐ Calm		
☐ Quiet		
☐ Restless		
☐ Anger		
☐ Anxious		
☐ Fearful		
☐ Other		

CARE NEEDS	TIME
Needed Help	

CARE NEEDS	TIME
Did themselves	

ACTIVITIES / TASKS	MEDICATION / TREATMENT NOTES
Successful	
Unsuccessful	
	OTHER NOTES / CONCERNS

DAILY REFLECTION	
What Worked? Positives	What Didn't Work? Negatives

Date

MOOD	TIME(S)	NOTES
☐ Happy		
☐ Grumpy		
☐ Tired		
☐ Energetic		
☐ Frustrated		
☐ Confused		
☐ Calm		
☐ Quiet		
☐ Restless		
☐ Anger		
☐ Anxious		
☐ Fearful		
☐ Other		

CARE NEEDS	TIME
Needed Help	

CARE NEEDS	TIME
Did themselves	

ACTIVITIES / TASKS

Successful

Unsuccessful

MEDICATION / TREATMENT NOTES

OTHER NOTES / CONCERNS

DAILY REFLECTION

What Worked? Positives	What Didn't Work? Negatives

Date

MOOD	TIME(S)	NOTES
☐ Happy		
☐ Grumpy		
☐ Tired		
☐ Energetic		
☐ Frustrated		
☐ Confused		
☐ Calm		
☐ Quiet		
☐ Restless		
☐ Anger		
☐ Anxious		
☐ Fearful		
☐ Other		

CARE NEEDS	TIME
Needed Help	

CARE NEEDS	TIME
Did themselves	

ACTIVITIES / TASKS

Successful

Unsuccessful

MEDICATION / TREATMENT NOTES

OTHER NOTES / CONCERNS

DAILY REFLECTION

What Worked? Positives	What Didn't Work? Negatives

Date

MOOD	TIME(S)	NOTES
☐ Happy		
☐ Grumpy		
☐ Tired		
☐ Energetic		
☐ Frustrated		
☐ Confused		
☐ Calm		
☐ Quiet		
☐ Restless		
☐ Anger		
☐ Anxious		
☐ Fearful		
☐ Other		

CARE NEEDS	TIME		CARE NEEDS	TIME
Needed Help			Did themselves	

ACTIVITIES / TASKS

Successful

Unsuccessful

MEDICATION / TREATMENT NOTES

OTHER NOTES / CONCERNS

DAILY REFLECTION

What Worked? Positives	What Didn't Work? Negatives

Weekly Recap & Patterns

MAIN MOOD(S) / TIMES / PATTERNS

CARE NEEDS PATTERNS

Needed Help

Did Themselves

WEEKLY ACTIVITIES / TASK PATTERNS

Successful

Unsuccessful

MEDICATION / TREATMENT NOTES

OTHER NOTES / WEEKLY CONCERNS

WEEKLY REFLECTION

What Worked? Positives	What Didn't Work? Negatives

Date

MOOD	TIME(S)	NOTES
☐ Happy		
☐ Grumpy		
☐ Tired		
☐ Energetic		
☐ Frustrated		
☐ Confused		
☐ Calm		
☐ Quiet		
☐ Restless		
☐ Anger		
☐ Anxious		
☐ Fearful		
☐ Other		

CARE NEEDS	TIME		CARE NEEDS	TIME
Needed Help			Did themselves	

ACTIVITIES / TASKS	MEDICATION / TREATMENT NOTES
Successful	
Unsuccessful	
	OTHER NOTES / CONCERNS

DAILY REFLECTION	
What Worked? Positives	**What Didn't Work? Negatives**

Date

MOOD	TIME(S)	NOTES
☐ Happy		
☐ Grumpy		
☐ Tired		
☐ Energetic		
☐ Frustrated		
☐ Confused		
☐ Calm		
☐ Quiet		
☐ Restless		
☐ Anger		
☐ Anxious		
☐ Fearful		
☐ Other		

CARE NEEDS	TIME
Needed Help	

CARE NEEDS	TIME
Did themselves	

ACTIVITIES / TASKS
Successful
Unsuccessful

MEDICATION / TREATMENT NOTES

OTHER NOTES / CONCERNS

DAILY REFLECTION	
What Worked? Positives	What Didn't Work? Negatives

Date

MOOD	TIME(S)	NOTES
☐ Happy		
☐ Grumpy		
☐ Tired		
☐ Energetic		
☐ Frustrated		
☐ Confused		
☐ Calm		
☐ Quiet		
☐ Restless		
☐ Anger		
☐ Anxious		
☐ Fearful		
☐ Other		

CARE NEEDS	TIME	CARE NEEDS	TIME
Needed Help		Did themselves	

ACTIVITIES / TASKS

Successful

Unsuccessful

MEDICATION / TREATMENT NOTES

OTHER NOTES / CONCERNS

DAILY REFLECTION

What Worked? Positives	What Didn't Work? Negatives

Date

MOOD	TIME(S)	NOTES
☐ Happy		
☐ Grumpy		
☐ Tired		
☐ Energetic		
☐ Frustrated		
☐ Confused		
☐ Calm		
☐ Quiet		
☐ Restless		
☐ Anger		
☐ Anxious		
☐ Fearful		
☐ Other		

CARE NEEDS	TIME
Needed Help	

CARE NEEDS	TIME
Did themselves	

ACTIVITIES / TASKS	MEDICATION / TREATMENT NOTES
Successful	
Unsuccessful	**OTHER NOTES / CONCERNS**

DAILY REFLECTION	
What Worked? Positives	**What Didn't Work? Negatives**

Date

MOOD	TIME(S)	NOTES
☐ Happy		
☐ Grumpy		
☐ Tired		
☐ Energetic		
☐ Frustrated		
☐ Confused		
☐ Calm		
☐ Quiet		
☐ Restless		
☐ Anger		
☐ Anxious		
☐ Fearful		
☐ Other		

CARE NEEDS	TIME
Needed Help	

CARE NEEDS	TIME
Did themselves	

ACTIVITIES / TASKS	MEDICATION / TREATMENT NOTES
Successful	
Unsuccessful	

	OTHER NOTES / CONCERNS

DAILY REFLECTION

What Worked? Positives	What Didn't Work? Negatives

Date

MOOD	TIME(S)	NOTES
☐ Happy		
☐ Grumpy		
☐ Tired		
☐ Energetic		
☐ Frustrated		
☐ Confused		
☐ Calm		
☐ Quiet		
☐ Restless		
☐ Anger		
☐ Anxious		
☐ Fearful		
☐ Other		

CARE NEEDS	TIME		CARE NEEDS	TIME
Needed Help			Did themselves	

ACTIVITIES / TASKS

Successful

Unsuccessful

MEDICATION / TREATMENT NOTES

OTHER NOTES / CONCERNS

DAILY REFLECTION

What Worked? Positives	What Didn't Work? Negatives

Date

MOOD	TIME(S)	NOTES
☐ Happy		
☐ Grumpy		
☐ Tired		
☐ Energetic		
☐ Frustrated		
☐ Confused		
☐ Calm		
☐ Quiet		
☐ Restless		
☐ Anger		
☐ Anxious		
☐ Fearful		
☐ Other		

CARE NEEDS	TIME
Needed Help	

CARE NEEDS	TIME
Did themselves	

ACTIVITIES / TASKS

Successful

Unsuccessful

MEDICATION / TREATMENT NOTES

OTHER NOTES / CONCERNS

DAILY REFLECTION

What Worked? Positives	What Didn't Work? Negatives

Weekly Recap & Patterns

MAIN MOOD(S) / TIMES / PATTERNS

CARE NEEDS PATTERNS
Needed Help
Did Themselves

WEEKLY ACTIVITIES / TASK PATTERNS	MEDICATION / TREATMENT NOTES
Successful	
Unsuccessful	**OTHER NOTES / WEEKLY CONCERNS**

WEEKLY REFLECTION	
What Worked? Positives	What Didn't Work? Negatives

Date

MOOD	TIME(S)	NOTES
☐ Happy		
☐ Grumpy		
☐ Tired		
☐ Energetic		
☐ Frustrated		
☐ Confused		
☐ Calm		
☐ Quiet		
☐ Restless		
☐ Anger		
☐ Anxious		
☐ Fearful		
☐ Other		

CARE NEEDS	TIME
Needed Help	

CARE NEEDS	TIME
Did themselves	

ACTIVITIES / TASKS	MEDICATION / TREATMENT NOTES
Successful	
Unsuccessful	

OTHER NOTES / CONCERNS

DAILY REFLECTION	
What Worked? Positives	**What Didn't Work? Negatives**

Date

MOOD	TIME(S)	NOTES
☐ Happy		
☐ Grumpy		
☐ Tired		
☐ Energetic		
☐ Frustrated		
☐ Confused		
☐ Calm		
☐ Quiet		
☐ Restless		
☐ Anger		
☐ Anxious		
☐ Fearful		
☐ Other		

CARE NEEDS	TIME
Needed Help	

CARE NEEDS	TIME
Did themselves	

ACTIVITIES / TASKS

Successful

Unsuccessful

MEDICATION / TREATMENT NOTES

OTHER NOTES / CONCERNS

DAILY REFLECTION

What Worked? Positives	What Didn't Work? Negatives

Date

MOOD	TIME(S)	NOTES
☐ Happy		
☐ Grumpy		
☐ Tired		
☐ Energetic		
☐ Frustrated		
☐ Confused		
☐ Calm		
☐ Quiet		
☐ Restless		
☐ Anger		
☐ Anxious		
☐ Fearful		
☐ Other		

CARE NEEDS	TIME	CARE NEEDS	TIME
Needed Help		Did themselves	

ACTIVITIES / TASKS	MEDICATION / TREATMENT NOTES
Successful	
Unsuccessful	
	OTHER NOTES / CONCERNS

DAILY REFLECTION	
What Worked? Positives	**What Didn't Work? Negatives**

Date

MOOD	TIME(S)	NOTES
☐ Happy		
☐ Grumpy		
☐ Tired		
☐ Energetic		
☐ Frustrated		
☐ Confused		
☐ Calm		
☐ Quiet		
☐ Restless		
☐ Anger		
☐ Anxious		
☐ Fearful		
☐ Other		

CARE NEEDS	TIME
Needed Help	

CARE NEEDS	TIME
Did themselves	

ACTIVITIES / TASKS

Successful

Unsuccessful

MEDICATION / TREATMENT NOTES

OTHER NOTES / CONCERNS

DAILY REFLECTION

What Worked? Positives	What Didn't Work? Negatives

Date

MOOD	TIME(S)	NOTES
☐ Happy		
☐ Grumpy		
☐ Tired		
☐ Energetic		
☐ Frustrated		
☐ Confused		
☐ Calm		
☐ Quiet		
☐ Restless		
☐ Anger		
☐ Anxious		
☐ Fearful		
☐ Other		

CARE NEEDS	TIME		CARE NEEDS	TIME
Needed Help			Did themselves	

ACTIVITIES / TASKS

Successful

Unsuccessful

MEDICATION / TREATMENT NOTES

OTHER NOTES / CONCERNS

DAILY REFLECTION

What Worked? Positives	What Didn't Work? Negatives

Date

MOOD	TIME(S)	NOTES
☐ Happy		
☐ Grumpy		
☐ Tired		
☐ Energetic		
☐ Frustrated		
☐ Confused		
☐ Calm		
☐ Quiet		
☐ Restless		
☐ Anger		
☐ Anxious		
☐ Fearful		
☐ Other		

CARE NEEDS	TIME
Needed Help	

CARE NEEDS	TIME
Did themselves	

ACTIVITIES / TASKS

Successful

Unsuccessful

MEDICATION / TREATMENT NOTES

OTHER NOTES / CONCERNS

DAILY REFLECTION

What Worked? Positives	What Didn't Work? Negatives

Date

MOOD	TIME(S)	NOTES
☐ Happy		
☐ Grumpy		
☐ Tired		
☐ Energetic		
☐ Frustrated		
☐ Confused		
☐ Calm		
☐ Quiet		
☐ Restless		
☐ Anger		
☐ Anxious		
☐ Fearful		
☐ Other		

CARE NEEDS	TIME
Needed Help	

CARE NEEDS	TIME
Did themselves	

ACTIVITIES / TASKS

Successful

Unsuccessful

MEDICATION / TREATMENT NOTES

OTHER NOTES / CONCERNS

DAILY REFLECTION

What Worked? Positives

What Didn't Work? Negatives

Weekly Recap & Patterns

MAIN MOOD(S) / TIMES / PATTERNS

CARE NEEDS PATTERNS

Needed Help

Did Themselves

WEEKLY ACTIVITIES / TASK PATTERNS

Successful

Unsuccessful

MEDICATION / TREATMENT NOTES

OTHER NOTES / WEEKLY CONCERNS

WEEKLY REFLECTION

What Worked? Positives	What Didn't Work? Negatives

Date

MOOD	TIME(S)	NOTES
☐ Happy		
☐ Grumpy		
☐ Tired		
☐ Energetic		
☐ Frustrated		
☐ Confused		
☐ Calm		
☐ Quiet		
☐ Restless		
☐ Anger		
☐ Anxious		
☐ Fearful		
☐ Other		

CARE NEEDS	TIME
Needed Help	

CARE NEEDS	TIME
Did themselves	

ACTIVITIES / TASKS	MEDICATION / TREATMENT NOTES
Successful	
Unsuccessful	
	OTHER NOTES / CONCERNS

DAILY REFLECTION	
What Worked? Positives	What Didn't Work? Negatives

Date

MOOD	TIME(S)	NOTES
☐ Happy		
☐ Grumpy		
☐ Tired		
☐ Energetic		
☐ Frustrated		
☐ Confused		
☐ Calm		
☐ Quiet		
☐ Restless		
☐ Anger		
☐ Anxious		
☐ Fearful		
☐ Other		

CARE NEEDS	TIME
Needed Help	

CARE NEEDS	TIME
Did themselves	

ACTIVITIES / TASKS	MEDICATION / TREATMENT NOTES
Successful	
Unsuccessful	
	OTHER NOTES / CONCERNS

DAILY REFLECTION	
What Worked? Positives	**What Didn't Work? Negatives**

Date

MOOD	TIME(S)	NOTES
☐ Happy		
☐ Grumpy		
☐ Tired		
☐ Energetic		
☐ Frustrated		
☐ Confused		
☐ Calm		
☐ Quiet		
☐ Restless		
☐ Anger		
☐ Anxious		
☐ Fearful		
☐ Other		

CARE NEEDS	TIME	CARE NEEDS	TIME
Needed Help		Did themselves	

ACTIVITIES / TASKS

Successful

Unsuccessful

MEDICATION / TREATMENT NOTES

OTHER NOTES / CONCERNS

DAILY REFLECTION

What Worked? Positives	What Didn't Work? Negatives

Date

MOOD	TIME(S)	NOTES
☐ Happy		
☐ Grumpy		
☐ Tired		
☐ Energetic		
☐ Frustrated		
☐ Confused		
☐ Calm		
☐ Quiet		
☐ Restless		
☐ Anger		
☐ Anxious		
☐ Fearful		
☐ Other		

CARE NEEDS	TIME
Needed Help	

CARE NEEDS	TIME
Did themselves	

ACTIVITIES / TASKS	MEDICATION / TREATMENT NOTES
Successful	
Unsuccessful	
	OTHER NOTES / CONCERNS

DAILY REFLECTION	
What Worked? Positives	**What Didn't Work? Negatives**

Date

MOOD	TIME(S)	NOTES
☐ Happy		
☐ Grumpy		
☐ Tired		
☐ Energetic		
☐ Frustrated		
☐ Confused		
☐ Calm		
☐ Quiet		
☐ Restless		
☐ Anger		
☐ Anxious		
☐ Fearful		
☐ Other		

CARE NEEDS	TIME
Needed Help	

CARE NEEDS	TIME
Did themselves	

ACTIVITIES / TASKS	MEDICATION / TREATMENT NOTES
Successful	
Unsuccessful	**OTHER NOTES / CONCERNS**

DAILY REFLECTION	
What Worked? Positives	What Didn't Work? Negatives

Date

MOOD	TIME(S)	NOTES
☐ Happy		
☐ Grumpy		
☐ Tired		
☐ Energetic		
☐ Frustrated		
☐ Confused		
☐ Calm		
☐ Quiet		
☐ Restless		
☐ Anger		
☐ Anxious		
☐ Fearful		
☐ Other		

CARE NEEDS	TIME
Needed Help	

CARE NEEDS	TIME
Did themselves	

ACTIVITIES / TASKS

Successful

Unsuccessful

MEDICATION / TREATMENT NOTES

OTHER NOTES / CONCERNS

DAILY REFLECTION

What Worked? Positives	What Didn't Work? Negatives

Date

MOOD	TIME(S)	NOTES
☐ Happy		
☐ Grumpy		
☐ Tired		
☐ Energetic		
☐ Frustrated		
☐ Confused		
☐ Calm		
☐ Quiet		
☐ Restless		
☐ Anger		
☐ Anxious		
☐ Fearful		
☐ Other		

CARE NEEDS	TIME
Needed Help	

CARE NEEDS	TIME
Did themselves	

ACTIVITIES / TASKS
Successful
Unsuccessful

MEDICATION / TREATMENT NOTES

OTHER NOTES / CONCERNS

DAILY REFLECTION	
What Worked? Positives	What Didn't Work? Negatives

Weekly Recap & Patterns

MAIN MOOD(S) / TIMES / PATTERNS

CARE NEEDS PATTERNS

Needed Help

Did Themselves

WEEKLY ACTIVITIES / TASK PATTERNS

Successful

Unsuccessful

MEDICATION / TREATMENT NOTES

OTHER NOTES / WEEKLY CONCERNS

WEEKLY REFLECTION

What Worked? Positives	What Didn't Work? Negatives

Date

MOOD	TIME(S)	NOTES
☐ Happy		
☐ Grumpy		
☐ Tired		
☐ Energetic		
☐ Frustrated		
☐ Confused		
☐ Calm		
☐ Quiet		
☐ Restless		
☐ Anger		
☐ Anxious		
☐ Fearful		
☐ Other		

CARE NEEDS	TIME
Needed Help	

CARE NEEDS	TIME
Did themselves	

ACTIVITIES / TASKS

Successful

Unsuccessful

MEDICATION / TREATMENT NOTES

OTHER NOTES / CONCERNS

DAILY REFLECTION

What Worked? Positives	What Didn't Work? Negatives

Date

MOOD	TIME(S)	NOTES
☐ Happy		
☐ Grumpy		
☐ Tired		
☐ Energetic		
☐ Frustrated		
☐ Confused		
☐ Calm		
☐ Quiet		
☐ Restless		
☐ Anger		
☐ Anxious		
☐ Fearful		
☐ Other		

CARE NEEDS	TIME		CARE NEEDS	TIME
Needed Help			Did themselves	

ACTIVITIES / TASKS	MEDICATION / TREATMENT NOTES
Successful	
Unsuccessful	

OTHER NOTES / CONCERNS

DAILY REFLECTION

What Worked? Positives	What Didn't Work? Negatives

Date

MOOD	TIME(S)	NOTES
☐ Happy		
☐ Grumpy		
☐ Tired		
☐ Energetic		
☐ Frustrated		
☐ Confused		
☐ Calm		
☐ Quiet		
☐ Restless		
☐ Anger		
☐ Anxious		
☐ Fearful		
☐ Other		

CARE NEEDS	TIME
Needed Help	

CARE NEEDS	TIME
Did themselves	

ACTIVITIES / TASKS	MEDICATION / TREATMENT NOTES
Successful	
Unsuccessful	
	OTHER NOTES / CONCERNS

DAILY REFLECTION	
What Worked? Positives	What Didn't Work? Negatives

Date

MOOD	TIME(S)	NOTES
☐ Happy		
☐ Grumpy		
☐ Tired		
☐ Energetic		
☐ Frustrated		
☐ Confused		
☐ Calm		
☐ Quiet		
☐ Restless		
☐ Anger		
☐ Anxious		
☐ Fearful		
☐ Other		

CARE NEEDS	TIME		CARE NEEDS	TIME
Needed Help			Did themselves	

ACTIVITIES / TASKS	MEDICATION / TREATMENT NOTES
Successful	
Unsuccessful	**OTHER NOTES / CONCERNS**

DAILY REFLECTION	
What Worked? Positives	**What Didn't Work? Negatives**

Date

MOOD	TIME(S)	NOTES
☐ Happy		
☐ Grumpy		
☐ Tired		
☐ Energetic		
☐ Frustrated		
☐ Confused		
☐ Calm		
☐ Quiet		
☐ Restless		
☐ Anger		
☐ Anxious		
☐ Fearful		
☐ Other		

CARE NEEDS	TIME
Needed Help	

CARE NEEDS	TIME
Did themselves	

ACTIVITIES / TASKS

Successful

Unsuccessful

MEDICATION / TREATMENT NOTES

OTHER NOTES / CONCERNS

DAILY REFLECTION

What Worked? Positives	What Didn't Work? Negatives

Date

MOOD	TIME(S)	NOTES
☐ Happy		
☐ Grumpy		
☐ Tired		
☐ Energetic		
☐ Frustrated		
☐ Confused		
☐ Calm		
☐ Quiet		
☐ Restless		
☐ Anger		
☐ Anxious		
☐ Fearful		
☐ Other		

CARE NEEDS	TIME
Needed Help	

CARE NEEDS	TIME
Did themselves	

ACTIVITIES / TASKS	MEDICATION / TREATMENT NOTES
Successful	
Unsuccessful	
	OTHER NOTES / CONCERNS

DAILY REFLECTION	
What Worked? Positives	**What Didn't Work? Negatives**

Date

MOOD	TIME(S)	NOTES
☐ Happy		
☐ Grumpy		
☐ Tired		
☐ Energetic		
☐ Frustrated		
☐ Confused		
☐ Calm		
☐ Quiet		
☐ Restless		
☐ Anger		
☐ Anxious		
☐ Fearful		
☐ Other		

CARE NEEDS	TIME
Needed Help	

CARE NEEDS	TIME
Did themselves	

ACTIVITIES / TASKS

Successful

Unsuccessful

MEDICATION / TREATMENT NOTES

OTHER NOTES / CONCERNS

DAILY REFLECTION

What Worked? Positives	What Didn't Work? Negatives

Weekly Recap & Patterns

MAIN MOOD(S) / TIMES / PATTERNS

CARE NEEDS PATTERNS

Needed Help

Did Themselves

WEEKLY ACTIVITIES / TASK PATTERNS

Successful

Unsuccessful

MEDICATION / TREATMENT NOTES

OTHER NOTES / WEEKLY CONCERNS

WEEKLY REFLECTION

What Worked? Positives	What Didn't Work? Negatives

Date

MOOD	TIME(S)	NOTES
☐ Happy		
☐ Grumpy		
☐ Tired		
☐ Energetic		
☐ Frustrated		
☐ Confused		
☐ Calm		
☐ Quiet		
☐ Restless		
☐ Anger		
☐ Anxious		
☐ Fearful		
☐ Other		

CARE NEEDS	TIME
Needed Help	

CARE NEEDS	TIME
Did themselves	

ACTIVITIES / TASKS

Successful

Unsuccessful

MEDICATION / TREATMENT NOTES

OTHER NOTES / CONCERNS

DAILY REFLECTION

What Worked? Positives	What Didn't Work? Negatives

Date

MOOD	TIME(S)	NOTES
☐ Happy		
☐ Grumpy		
☐ Tired		
☐ Energetic		
☐ Frustrated		
☐ Confused		
☐ Calm		
☐ Quiet		
☐ Restless		
☐ Anger		
☐ Anxious		
☐ Fearful		
☐ Other		

CARE NEEDS	TIME
Needed Help	

CARE NEEDS	TIME
Did themselves	

ACTIVITIES / TASKS

Successful

Unsuccessful

MEDICATION / TREATMENT NOTES

OTHER NOTES / CONCERNS

DAILY REFLECTION

What Worked? Positives	What Didn't Work? Negatives

Date

MOOD	TIME(S)	NOTES
☐ Happy		
☐ Grumpy		
☐ Tired		
☐ Energetic		
☐ Frustrated		
☐ Confused		
☐ Calm		
☐ Quiet		
☐ Restless		
☐ Anger		
☐ Anxious		
☐ Fearful		
☐ Other		

CARE NEEDS	TIME
Needed Help	

CARE NEEDS	TIME
Did themselves	

ACTIVITIES / TASKS	MEDICATION / TREATMENT NOTES
Successful	
Unsuccessful	
	OTHER NOTES / CONCERNS

DAILY REFLECTION	
What Worked? Positives	What Didn't Work? Negatives

Date

MOOD	TIME(S)	NOTES
☐ Happy		
☐ Grumpy		
☐ Tired		
☐ Energetic		
☐ Frustrated		
☐ Confused		
☐ Calm		
☐ Quiet		
☐ Restless		
☐ Anger		
☐ Anxious		
☐ Fearful		
☐ Other		

CARE NEEDS	TIME
Needed Help	

CARE NEEDS	TIME
Did themselves	

ACTIVITIES / TASKS	MEDICATION / TREATMENT NOTES
Successful	
Unsuccessful	

OTHER NOTES / CONCERNS

DAILY REFLECTION

What Worked? Positives	What Didn't Work? Negatives

Date

MOOD	TIME(S)	NOTES
☐ Happy		
☐ Grumpy		
☐ Tired		
☐ Energetic		
☐ Frustrated		
☐ Confused		
☐ Calm		
☐ Quiet		
☐ Restless		
☐ Anger		
☐ Anxious		
☐ Fearful		
☐ Other		

CARE NEEDS	TIME
Needed Help	

CARE NEEDS	TIME
Did themselves	

ACTIVITIES / TASKS	MEDICATION / TREATMENT NOTES
Successful	
Unsuccessful	**OTHER NOTES / CONCERNS**

DAILY REFLECTION	
What Worked? Positives	**What Didn't Work? Negatives**

Date

MOOD	TIME(S)	NOTES
☐ Happy		
☐ Grumpy		
☐ Tired		
☐ Energetic		
☐ Frustrated		
☐ Confused		
☐ Calm		
☐ Quiet		
☐ Restless		
☐ Anger		
☐ Anxious		
☐ Fearful		
☐ Other		

CARE NEEDS	TIME
Needed Help	

CARE NEEDS	TIME
Did themselves	

ACTIVITIES / TASKS	MEDICATION / TREATMENT NOTES
Successful	
Unsuccessful	
	OTHER NOTES / CONCERNS

DAILY REFLECTION	
What Worked? Positives	**What Didn't Work? Negatives**

Date

MOOD	TIME(S)	NOTES
☐ Happy		
☐ Grumpy		
☐ Tired		
☐ Energetic		
☐ Frustrated		
☐ Confused		
☐ Calm		
☐ Quiet		
☐ Restless		
☐ Anger		
☐ Anxious		
☐ Fearful		
☐ Other		

CARE NEEDS	TIME		CARE NEEDS	TIME
Needed Help			Did themselves	

ACTIVITIES / TASKS

Successful

Unsuccessful

MEDICATION / TREATMENT NOTES

OTHER NOTES / CONCERNS

DAILY REFLECTION

What Worked? Positives	What Didn't Work? Negatives

Weekly Recap & Patterns

MAIN MOOD(S) / TIMES / PATTERNS

CARE NEEDS PATTERNS

Needed Help

Did Themselves

WEEKLY ACTIVITIES / TASK PATTERNS

Successful

Unsuccessful

MEDICATION / TREATMENT NOTES

OTHER NOTES / WEEKLY CONCERNS

WEEKLY REFLECTION

What Worked? Positives	What Didn't Work? Negatives

Date

MOOD	TIME(S)	NOTES
☐ Happy		
☐ Grumpy		
☐ Tired		
☐ Energetic		
☐ Frustrated		
☐ Confused		
☐ Calm		
☐ Quiet		
☐ Restless		
☐ Anger		
☐ Anxious		
☐ Fearful		
☐ Other		

CARE NEEDS	TIME		CARE NEEDS	TIME
Needed Help			Did themselves	

ACTIVITIES / TASKS	MEDICATION / TREATMENT NOTES
Successful	
Unsuccessful	

OTHER NOTES / CONCERNS

DAILY REFLECTION	
What Worked? Positives	What Didn't Work? Negatives

Made in the USA
Las Vegas, NV
25 October 2022

58156513R00085